WHY DO STARS TWINKLE?

BY ISAAC ASIMOV

Gareth Stevens Children's Books
MILWAUKEE

For a free color catalog describing Gareth Stevens' list of high-quality children's books, call 1-800-341-3569 (USA) or 1-800-461-9120 (Canada).

Library of Congress Cataloging-in-Publication Data

Asimov, Isaac, 1920-
    Why do stars twinkle? / by Isaac Asimov. — A Gareth Stevens Children's Books ed.
       p. cm. — (Ask Isaac Asimov)
    Includes bibliographical references and index.
    Summary: Explains why stars in the night sky appear to twinkle.
    ISBN 0-8368-0437-6
    1. Stars—Juvenile literature. [1. Stars.] I. Title. II. Series: Asimov, Isaac, 1920-
Ask Isaac Asimov.
QB801.7.A86 1991
523.8—dc20   90-25921

A Gareth Stevens Children's Books edition

Edited, designed, and produced by
Gareth Stevens Children's Books
1555 North RiverCenter Drive, Suite 201
Milwaukee, Wisconsin 53212, USA

Picture Credits
Paul Dimare, pp. 8-9; Gareth Stevens, Inc., © 1989, p. 17 (inset); Paul H. Henning/Third Coast, © 1983, pp. 10-11; Rick Karpinski/DeWalt and Associates, pp. 4-5; © Fred Klein, pp. 18-19; Mark Maxwell, pp. 14-15; Mark Mille/ DeWalt and Associates, pp. 12-13; NASA, pp. 6-7, 20-21; National Optical Astronomy Observatories, cover, pp. 16-17, 24; © NRAO/AUI, p. 19 (inset); © Frank Zullo, pp. 22-23

Series editor: Elizabeth Kaplan
Editor: Kelli Peduzzi
Series designer: Sabine Huschke
Picture researcher: Daniel Helminak
Consulting editor: Matthew Groshek

Printed in MEXICO

1 2 3 4 5 6 7 8 9 97 96 95 94 93 92 91

Contents

Words that appear in the glossary are printed in **boldface** type the
first time they occur in the text.

A World of Questions

Our world is full of strange and beautiful things, such as the night sky glimmering with **stars**. Sometimes we have questions about the things we see around us. Asking questions helps us appreciate the wonders of the Universe.

For instance, when you watch the stars on a clear, dark night, do you notice that they flicker? We say that the stars are **twinkling**. The twinkling stars look like tiny, beautiful jewels. But *why* do they twinkle? Let's find out.

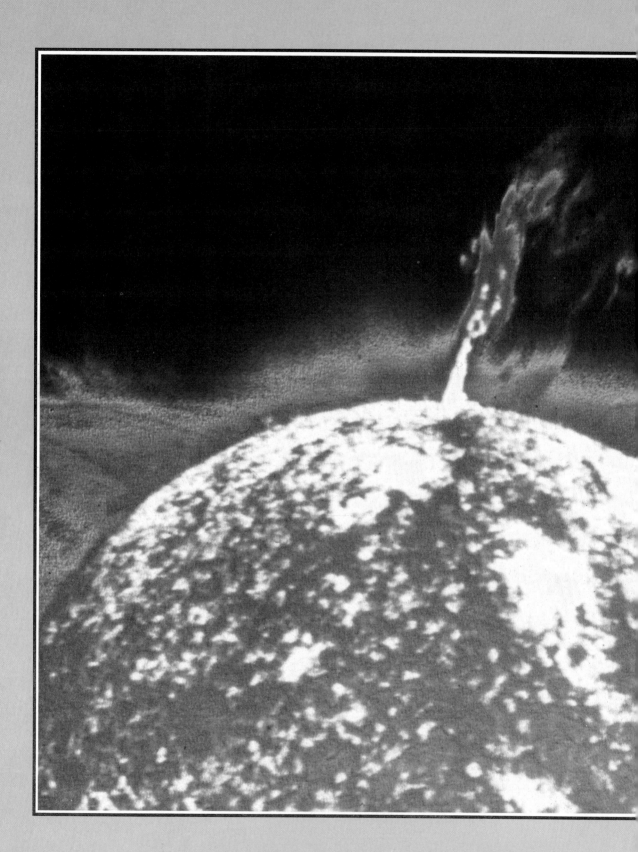

The Sun, the Stars, the Light

Stars are huge globes of hot gas. They send their light and heat out into space. The star nearest to us is the Sun. It is 93 million miles (150 million km) away. Yet it is close enough for us to feel its warmth.

The Sun is just an average-sized star. Yet to us, it looks like a huge disk of light in the sky. Compared to the Sun, other stars look like tiny specks of light.

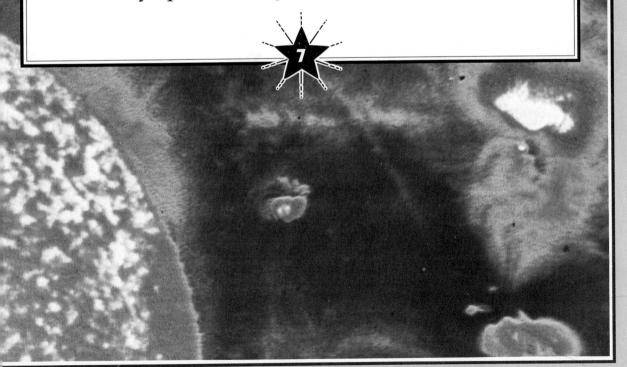

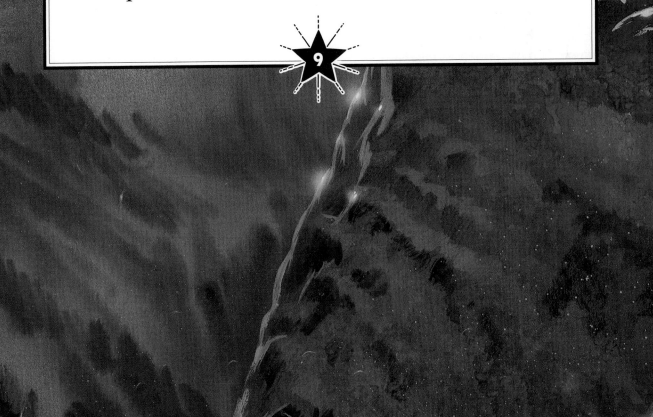

The Faraway Stars

Other stars are much farther away from us than the Sun is. They are so far away that we see them only as tiny points of light. During the daytime, the bright light from the Sun drowns them out. We can see the stars' light only at night.

The gleaming dot of light in this picture is what the Sun would look like from the planet Pluto, shown here with its moon, Charon. From Pluto, the Sun would be too far away to brighten the sky and to warm the planet.

9

Light that Fools the Eye

Starlight comes straight to us from far away, but its long journey ends with strange twists and turns. In fact, twinkling stars are not really changing brightness at all. They just look as if they are! Twinkling is an **optical illusion**, something that looks real but isn't.

10

We can see another optical illusion. As we travel along on a hot, sunny day, we may see what looks like water shimmering on the road ahead. But when we get up close, the water isn't there! This optical illusion happens for the same reason that stars appear to twinkle.

Bending Light

Shimmering pavement? Twinkling stars? Both of these optical illusions happen because of the way light travels. Most of the time, it travels in a straight line. But light will bend when it passes through layers of hot and cold air.

12

On warm days, the layers of air near the ground become hotter than the layers that are higher up. When light passes through the hot air, then through the cool air, it bends. To the eye, the bending light makes the pavement look as if it is rippling.

13

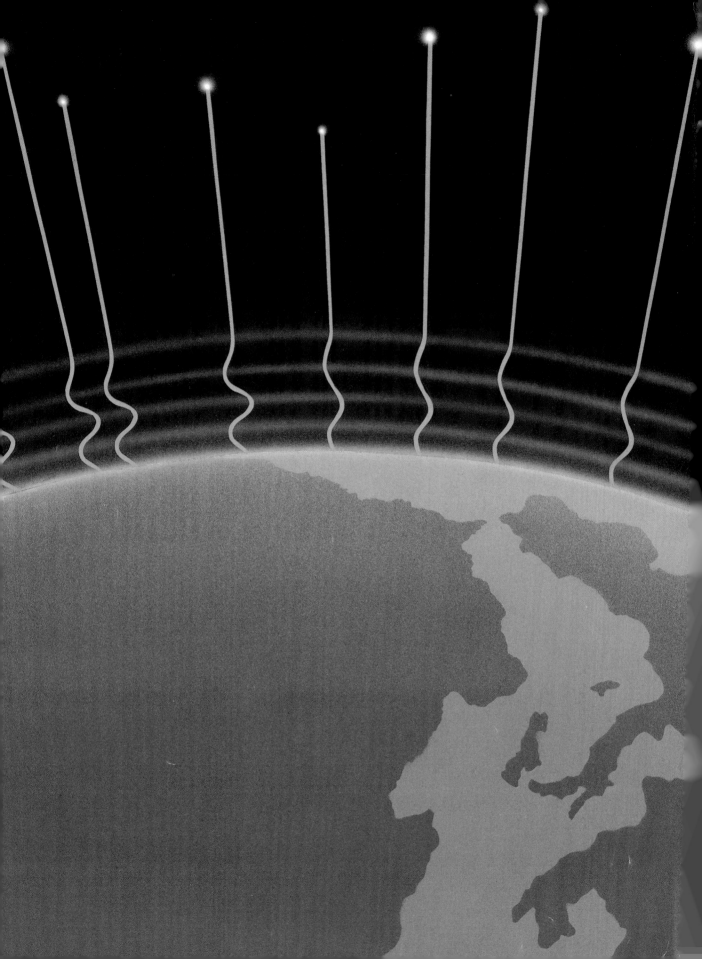

Starlight Bends, Too

Starlight also passes through layers of hot and cold air in Earth's atmosphere. As starlight passes through these layers, it bends. When we see the stars twinkling, it's really the starlight bending as it passes through the air.

Stars twinkle more in the early evening, when warm air rises from the ground. If you live in a place where day and night temperatures are very different, you will also see more twinkling.

15

The Tricky Twinkling

Astronomers use **telescopes** to look at the stars. A telescope makes the stars look larger and brighter than they appear to the naked eye. An astronomer gets a closer look at the stars with a telescope, but the twinkling looks even stronger, too.

This makes stargazing tricky for astronomers. They want to be able to see the stars clearly, but the twinkling makes the stars fade in and out. Astronomers need the starlight to remain steady so they can study the stars.

A Better Look at the Stars

Astronomers have found ways to get a better look at the stars. To lessen the twinkling, they put telescopes high in the mountains, where the air is cold and clear. They also put telescopes near the ocean, where the day and night temperatures are fairly steady.

Astronomers also use computers to see the stars. A computer helps a telescope to focus on a star using special **lasers** and mirrors. Then the computer takes what the telescope sees and turns it into pictures on the screen. All this helps astronomers look at the stars.

The Hubble Space Telescope — Our Eye to the Stars

The best way to observe the stars is to get above the air. **Astronauts** traveling in space see the stars shining steadily. In space, stars don't twinkle! This is because space has no air. Without air, starlight travels straight through space without bending.

In 1990, scientists put the **Hubble Space Telescope** into orbit around Earth. They hoped that the telescope would take clearer pictures of the stars. Unfortunately, the Hubble's mirror has a flaw. It has not allowed astronomers to see the stars as well as they had hoped. But the telescope is still taking clearer pictures of stars than we could get from Earth.

Many More Questions about Stars

Even though the twinkling of the stars is an optical illusion, it is still beautiful. We never tire of looking at the stars twinkling in the darkness, and we can't help wondering more about them. How many stars exist? Are there different kinds of stars? Will we ever be able to travel to the stars? The questions we can ask about stars are almost as numerous as the stars themselves. Future astronomers will find even more questions to ask — and to answer.

More Books about Stars

All About Stars by Lawrence Jefferies (Troll)
Discovering the Stars by Laurence Santrey (Troll)
The Sky is Full of Stars by Franklyn M. Branley (Crowell Junior Books)
The Space Spotter's Guide by Isaac Asimov (Gareth Stevens)
Stars by Phoebe Crosby (Garrard)
Sun and Stars by Norman Barrett (Franklin Watts)

Places to Write

If you want to find out more about stars, here are some places to write to for more information. Be sure to ask exactly what you want to know about. Include your age, full name, address, and an envelope with a stamp on it so they can write back to you.

Stardate
McDonald Observatory
Austin, Texas 78712

NASA Jet Propulsion
   Laboratory
Public Affairs 180-201
4800 Oak Grove Drive
Pasadena, California 91109

National Museum of Science
   and Technology
Astronomy Division
2380 Lancaster Road
Ottawa, Ontario K1A 0M8

Glossary

astronaut (ASS-trow-nawt): a person trained to fly spacecraft or who travels in a spacecraft.

astronomer (ass-TRON-uh-mer): a person who studies and observes the stars, the planets, and other space objects.

Hubble Space Telescope (HUH-bull SPACE TELL-uh-scope): the powerful telescope in orbit around Earth that scientists hope will help them see very distant stars and other space objects.

laser (LAY-zer): a device that gathers radiation and other types of energy and changes them into a powerful beam of light.

optical illusion (AHP-tih-kuhl ih-LOO-zhun): anything that appears to be visible to the eye, but in fact is not real.

star (STAHR): a giant globe of gas that sends out light, heat, and radiation into space.

telescope (TELL-uh-scope): a device that uses lenses and mirrors to observe distant objects in space.

twinkling (TWINK-ling): flickering and shimmering, as a star does in the night sky.

Index